Franklin Watts Inc
387 Park Avenue South
New York NY 10016

Library of Congress Cataloging-in-Publication Data
Barrett, Norman S.
    The picture world of sea rescue / Norman Barrett.
        p.   cm. — (Picture world)
    Summary: Examines vehicles and methods used for emergency rescue
operations at sea, discussing tugboats, hovercraft, flying boats,
and icebreakers.
    ISBN 0–531–14093–8
    1. Life-saving—Juvenile literature.   2. Life-boats—Juvenile
literature.   3. Search and rescue operations—Juvenile literature.
[1. Search and rescue operations.]   I. Title.   II. Series.
VK1473.B37   1991
363.12'3—dc20   90–31019
                                                        CIP AC

Designed by
K and Co

Photographs by
RNLI (John Dodds, Dave Trotter,
    A.M. Ferry, Ambrose
    Greenway)
U.S. Coast Guard
Canadian Coastguard
RAF High Wycombe
Australian Overseas Information
    Service, London
U.S. Navy
Norman Barrett
Hull Daily Mail
Cleveland County Fire Brigade
RGIT Survival Centre, Aberdeen
Sikorsky Aircraft
Elvin Wood of Humber Tugs
Paul Berriff Productions in
    association with Scottish TV

Technical Consultant
RNLI

The Picture World of
Sea Rescue

Norman Barrett

CONTENTS

Franklin Watts

New York • London • Sydney • Toronto

Introduction

Rescue organizations use lifeboats and helicopters to save people in trouble at sea.

They might come to the aid of lone sailors whose boat has capsized or the crew of an oil tanker on fire.

Lifeboats range from small inflatable dinghies to 60 meter (200 ft) cutters.

Helicopters can hover over the waves as they hoist people to safety.

▽ A lifeboat sets out in rough seas. Most rescues take place in bad weather. The brave men who crew the boats are members of the Coast Guard search and rescue operations.

◁ A helicopter hovers over a lifeboat as the hoistman does his work. People may be hoisted onto or off boats during a rescue operation.

▷ Lifeboatmen take part in a rescue exercise. The crew is trained in basic medical techniques and can give emergency care to victims on the way back to shore.

Lifeboats

There are lifeboat stations at intervals along the coast of many countries. Different kinds of lifeboats are used, depending on the coastal conditions they work in. Some lifeboats operate close to the shore, while others have to go far out to sea.

Launching methods vary, too. Special methods are called for when launching from cliffs or rocky bays.

▽ An Arun class lifeboat is about 16 m (52–54 ft) long and has a crew of six or seven. Lifeboats must be strong enough to go to sea in all kinds of weather. They must be small enough to get close to wrecks or to big ships in trouble. They have a powerful radio and equipment for navigation.

△ Lifeboat equipment includes stretchers, lifejackets, lifebelts, oars, ropes, a compass, flashlights, a first aid kit, breathing apparatus, drugs and medicines, and other special survival gear and tools.

△ Tractors may be used for launching lifeboats from sandy beaches. The tractor pulls the lifeboat from the boathouse to the beach on a trailer, and then to the water's edge, before going around to the back and pushing it into the water.

◁ A lifeboat is launched from steep cliffs down a special slipway.

Lifeboats are built to avoid capsizing, but they are also designed to be self-righting in case they do.

△ A lifeboat is pulled over in a self-righting test.

▽ The lifeboat does not stay overturned, but springs back to an upright position.

Rescue!

▽ A blazing oil tanker dwarfs the Humber lifeboat (seen on the right), which came to its rescue off the English coast.

▷ Crew of the oil tanker on the deck of the lifeboat after being taken off their burning ship.

▽ A fire tug finishes the job, spraying water on the tanker after the fire has been put out with foam.

Inshore craft

Smaller craft are used for inshore duties. Inflatable lifeboats and hovercraft can work close to the shore and near sandbanks. Fast and maneuverable, they may be launched quickly from the shore.

Inflatable lifeboats may also be carried on larger boats. These small rescue craft now save more lives than the seagoing boats. They are used to rescue swimmers or surfers in trouble, or dinghies that have capsized or been swept out to sea.

△ A "C" class lifeboat is only 5.3 m (17.5 ft) long but has a speed of 27 knots (50 km/h). It has an outboard motor, and its hull is made of reinforced nylon.

△ Divers work from a hovercraft of the Canadian Coast Guard. These air cushion vehicles operate in areas of drying mud flats, strong tidal rapids, and whirlpools, where both fishing and pleasure boats get into difficulties.

◁ A pilot at the controls of a hovercraft.

15

△ The U.S. Coast Guard operates small inflatable craft off the coast of California.

▽ Lifesavers on Sydney's Bondi Beach, Australia, bring their surf rescue craft ashore.

Fire boats

Lifeboats carry fire
fighting equipment, but
special fire boats, big
and small, are often
needed to tackle fires
at sea.

▷ An inflatable fire
rescue dinghy of a fire
brigade in northern
England.

▽ A Canadian Coast
Guard fire boat turns
its powerful jets on a
fire at sea.

17

Planes and helicopters

Aircraft are used at sea in search and rescue operations. Planes are used mainly for searching wide areas, although seaplanes can land on the water.

Helicopters are quick to get to the scene of an emergency. They can land on ships or they can hover in the air and pick up survivors from small craft or directly from the sea.

△ A plane of the Royal Air Force on search and rescue patrol. In many countries search and rescue operations are carried out by aircraft of the armed forces. Some countries have coast guards with their own planes and helicopters.

△ A Sikorsky helicopter of the U.S. Coast Guard on patrol.

◁ Hoisting up a crew member from a ship that has gone aground in treacherous waters. Survivors may be transferred to the lifeboat on the left, which cannot get any closer to the ship.

◁ Taking a person off a boat, the hoistman secures him in a harness and then holds him steady as the hoist operator winds them up.

▽ The hoist operator's view as the hoistman takes a cradle down to a life raft.

A typical rescue helicopter has a pilot, a copilot, a hoistman, and a radar operator who also operates the hoist. The hoist is a long wire wound around a drum. It operates from the main cabin door and is worked electrically.

The hoist operator can maneuver the helicopter into the best position for hoisting as it hovers about 12–15 m (40–50 ft) above the sea.

△ The scene over the North Sea after the Piper Alpha oil platform explosion in 1988. Every available helicopter rushed to the disaster to ferry survivors to the hospital.

◁ A badly burned casualty is hoisted up in a stretcher to a helicopter from an oil rig support ship.

▷ A fire fighting and rescue drill on board an amphibious assault ship. Crash crewmen in fire-resistant suits prepare to remove crewmen from an Iroquois helicopter.

▽ A Sea King hovers over a pilot who has crashed after being launched from an aircraft carrier.

23

Underwater rescue

Divers sometimes become trapped underwater, or a submarine gets into difficulties and sinks or cannot surface. Special methods are needed for underwater rescue.

Craft called submersibles are used for underwater rescue work. Robot search vehicles are used as well as manned submersibles. They are usually operated from a ship on the surface, although one type is carried on a submarine.

△ A deep submergence rescue vehicle (DSRV) is carried down by a submarine to a submarine in need of assistance. It can rescue 24 crew members at a time.

Survival capsules

Special survival craft are used on oil drilling platforms, where fire and gas fumes might endanger survivors in an open boat.

These survival capsules are totally enclosed and are motor-propelled. They are made of fiberglass and have their own oxygen system.

▽ Oil platform survival capsules can carry 50 people away from a fire in safety, before being picked up by a rescue boat.

25

Rescue training

Both lifeboat and helicopter crews undergo training for their duties. While saving the lives of others, they often put their own lives at risk, and mistakes can be fatal. The various lifesaving procedures may be learned and practiced at special training centers.

△ Rescue procedures are practiced at a survival training center. The water is whipped up by wind and wave making machines as an exercise with inflatable life rafts is performed.

The first lifeboats

Heroic stories of rescues at sea have been told for as long as people have gone out in boats. The first lifeboats, though, were not built until the 1790s, in England, and were rowed by 10 oarsmen.

The seas around the British Isles can be among the roughest in the world. In 1824, a voluntary organization was set up for "the preservation of life from shipwreck," becoming the Royal National Lifeboat Institution (RNLI) in 1854.

△ A painting before the age of motorboats shows a lifeboat of the RNLI sailing off after rescuing survivors of a shipwreck.

The U.S. Coast Guard

The U.S. government has operated the lifesaving services in the United States since 1871. The U.S. Coast Guard was formed in 1951, when the Lifesaving Service was combined with the

Revenue Cutter Service, a fleet that patrolled the coasts to prevent smuggling and protect merchant vessels.

The Fastnet rescue
The Fastnet Race is an annual international long-distance yacht race held in waters off the British Isles. The people who take part in this event are expert sailors and rarely need assistance. But the 1979 race was an exception, as terrible storms whipped up the waves and tossed the boats all over the place.

The rescue operation was made more difficult because of the small size of the craft spread over a wide area, many without radio. Several people died, but the combined operation of helicopters, lifeboats, and other vessels rescued 139.

Abandon ship!
Ships have their own lifeboats for passengers and crew in case of emergencies. If the cry "Abandon ship!" goes out, there are lifejackets for all the people on board, and they take to the lifeboats which can be quickly lowered over the sides.

△ A lifeboat comes to the rescue of a yacht in distress during the Fastnet Race of 1979.

△ A passenger liner's lifeboats are ready to be lowered into the water in an emergency.

Glossary

Capsize
A capsized ship is one that has overturned.

Cutter
One of the larger types of ships used by coast guards.

Hoist
An instrument used to lower and raise people or things from a helicopter. It consists of a strong line wound onto a drum. The drum is turned to let the line in or out.

Hoistman
The person who goes down on the hoist line during rescue operations.

Hovercraft
A craft that forces out a layer of air at the bottom for it to travel on. Hovercraft, also called air cushion vehicles, can travel over both land and water.

Inflatable
Able to be filled or pumped up with air or another gas.

Lifebelt
A floating ring, or life preserver in the shape of a belt, used for aiding survival in the water.

Lifeboat
A special rescue boat ready to go to sea in an emergency.

Lifejacket
An inflatable jacket worn to keep a person afloat in the water.

Radar
A means of sending out special radio waves to detect objects at a distance. Radar is used at sea and in the air for search and rescue operations.

Self-righting
Most lifeboats are designed to be self-righting, so that if they overturn they come straight back up again.

Submersible
A craft used for underwater operations.

Index